Floristic•
Basics

Floristic•
Basics

Gudrun Cottenier & Nico Bostoen

Photography:
Isabelle Persyn

stichting
kunstboek

Introduction

Dear reader,

Making this book has been quite a challenge. From a didactic point of view, we always try to work constructively. First and foremost it's our goal to teach techniques, instead of making just one specific floral arrangement. We want to enable our students to use the techniques in order to make other arrangements themselves.

While we were thinking about the contents and shape of this book, we were able to structuralise the flower arranging techniques, mainly based on our experience (more than twenty years!) and vision. Having said this, we definitely don't want to pretend we have made a comprehensive work. Techniques and materials are furthermore subject to a continuous evolution. Every technique is presented in a short text and is complemented with a number of possibilities and tips. A step by step example illustrates the technique, followed by a number of floral arrangements. In a separate chapter you will find out more about the materials, the care for floral materials, the style in floristry, how to choose colours and shapes and also how and when floristry came into existence.

We hope that looking through this book will give you more 'technical' insights into your own floral works. It would be fantastic if this book enables you to analyse the floral arrangements you come across. They can be an inspiration for your own designs.

In a book on the basic flower arranging techniques, we would also

like to answer two essential questions: What is a flower arrangement? and Why are people so keen on producing floral creations?
For the first question, I searched for an explanation in the dictionary (in this case the *Longman Contemporary English*) and tried to express my own vision.
According to the dictionary: the aesthetic arranging of flowers in vases and containers.
According to Gudrun: the making of creative compositions with natural materials: flowers, leaves and fruits.

Our experience and contact with our students have given us a long list of answers to the second question. First of all people cannot live without flowers or plants. They adorn our gardens and give colour — and often a nice fragrance — to our homes. For many people flower arranging and gardening are beautiful professions or an entertaining hobby.
Additionally interior decoration has become increasingly more important and flowers should be part of every interior. A floral creation undoubtedly gives our interior design added value.
Flower arranging is more and more considered as an art form, closely connected to architecture, painting, sculpture, photography, landscaping and culinary art. Moreover, it is often inspired by other art forms. Floral art is very subject to trends. There is a constant evolution in the use of materials, the combinations and the techniques. This makes it so fascinating, that you will always want to learn more!
Working with plant material is very relaxing. You have to concentrate on the preparation of the materials and the design. Being involved in a creative activity relieves your thoughts from all daily worries. When you are arranging flowers all your senses are stimulated: you observe the colours, smell the scent and feel the texture ...

Before you start your creation, it is good to draw a sketch of what you have in mind. Dedicate sufficient time and attention to the preparations, like gathering the material and choosing the right surface. Nevertheless, contrary to other activities, flower arranging is a hobby that allows you to make creations relatively quickly. Anyone who is interested and has sufficient patience can learn. Besides, practice makes perfect! If you manage to develop your own style and other people can recognise your work among others', then you are really on the right path.

We hope that you find tons of knowledge and inspiration in this book and we wish you a lot of success!

Gudrun Cottenier & Nico Bostoen

Contents

Sticking

According to the dictionary:
1 to push (a pointed object) into or through something
— **2** to (cause to) be fixed (as if) with a sticky substance
— **3** to become fixed in position, not move

According to Gudrun:
To stick vegetable materials in or onto a base

Possibilities:

- Although sticking is a very old technique, it is still used a lot in trendy and classical arrangements, e.g. wreaths, garlands, table decorations, wall ornaments, etc.
- When the materials you use need water, e.g. flowers, greenery ..., you can use floral foam for the base. Floral foam as we know it today is a relatively young product. But you can also use traditional base materials, e.g. clay (I recommend you knead it thoroughly with water), sphagnum or peat moss. These materials are also much more environment-friendly.
- Materials that don't need water can be bound onto wire, pricked on sticks, etc. and then stuck into polystyrene, grey floral foam or other base materials. As a consequence the sticking technique is suitable for both fresh and dry or dried materials, e.g. lyophilised (freeze-dried) or stabilised materials.
- Sticking is often used to complement other techniques: a garland or festoon is basically bound, but you can stick materials in between or at the ends. Other possibilities are e.g. to glue cinnamon sticks onto a frame and to create a fine arrangement using that shape with flowers and greenery and using the sticking technique.
- Sticking is extremely popular among flower arrangers for the creation of Biedermeiers. This makes a nice, even distribution of all the materials on a half-ball. You can also stick the materials in small groups, sorting them by type or species.

Tips:

- Wet floral foam is sturdier than dry green floral foam.
- Before you stick the flowers and the greenery onto the base, it is important to carefully cut the material and tear off all small, thin leaves or sprigs to avoid getting them into the floral foam.
- First the flowers or the greenery? Professional florists often start with the greenery and then add the flowers for practical reasons: greenery lasts much longer than flowers. When you have to produce many arrangements, it is recommended to leave the material that wilts the fastest aside and arrange it at the end. However, much depends also on the sturdiness of the stems. If you are using flowers with weak stems, I recommend you arrange them before you start with the greenery. Personally, I often prefer to start with the flowers because this way you can place them exactly where you want them. As you can see, both methods have advantages and disadvantages.
- Mark out the shape of your composition with flowers or greenery. This is more recommended than going piece by piece. If you mark out the big lines first, you have a better view of where you are going to. The final result will look much better.
- I recommend you attach a wire to materials with a weak stem, e.g. Gypsophila, Hydrangea ... This way it will be easier to stick them into the floral foam. You can also bind or prick the materials onto a stick or floral wire, e.g. prick ornamental apples on a stick, bind pinecones, etc.

Step by step

> **Materials:**
Rosmarinus officinalis, Lavandula angustifolia, Muscari, Buxus, Lamium (dead nettle)

1| Cover the inside of a square zinc container with plastic film. Place the wet floral foam on top of the plastic. Level off the edges of the floral foam to obtain a nicer final result.

2| Finish the inside with flat moss. Attach the moss with greening pins.

3| Cut green material, e.g. rosemary, lavender, boxwood and dead nettle very short. Remove the foliage and prick the branches (without the leaves) into the floral foam. This way you will be able to fill the floral foam in a much denser, compacter way. This is very important when the material starts drying.

4| Distribute the Muscari flowers over the arrangement.

Tip: It is not always easy to prick thin stems into wet floral foam. Make a small hole with a skewer first.

Take a small candle in a glass jar and place it in the middle of the square. The arrangement will look much nicer if you put a dish underneath.

Glass in clay

Cover a dish with a thick layer of modelling clay. Stick glass tubes into the clay, forming a circle. Now stick pulp cane branches crosswise into the clay. Arrange Ornithogalum arabicum in the glass tubes. The small Meulenbeckia twigs create a fresh effect.

Spring dish

Place a moss-covered wreath on a dish. Arrange a moss-covered polystyrene half-ball in the middle of the wreath. Attach irregular pieces of fruit tree branches with long greening pins. Fill the plastic tubes, nicely hidden in the moss, with Ornitogalum arabicum and green turban buttercups (Ranunculus inra 'Success Green'). To avoid monotony use Iceland moss, attached with greening pins. Finish the arrangement with eggshells.

Rose arch

Pack the vase with wet floral foam. Make an arch with chicken wire and wet floral foam. Attach the arch to the vase with skewers. Do not overlap the chicken wire too much, otherwise it will be very difficult to introduce the rose stems. Combine different coloured roses.

Romantic tuft basket

Wrap the handle of the basket in small hydrangea tufts with thin winding wire. Lay a long dish with floral foam in the basket. Fill with all kinds of summer materials, e.g. Malus apples, Hydrangea, roses (Rosa), unripe elderberries (Sambucus nigra), Hedera helix, Pyracantha berries and love-in-a-mist (Nigella damascena).

Monotonous simplicity

Fill a long dish with wet floral foam. Prick short stems of Chrysanthemum 'Santine Madilou White' in the foam.

This chrysanthemum variety is very similar to marguerite.

Lay flexible, paper thread randomly over the arrangement. The Meulenbeckia vines give a very fresh touch.

According to the dictionary:

Thread: **1** (a line of) very thin cord made by spinning cotton, wool, silk, etc., used in sewing or weaving — **2** a line of reasoning connecting the parts of an argument or story
Techniques: **1** method of doing or creating something that needs skill, esp. in art, music, literature, etc.

According to Gudrun:

To attach natural materials using thread or wire, in order to give them more sturdiness. This way, they can be used for multiple purposes.

Possibilities:

It is impossible to think of contemporary floral arranging without wire techniques. Many people think the use of wire is very artificial and it takes away the flowers' natural aspect, but it does offer lots of possibilities. It gives the material additional support and allows you to force it into a certain position.

On the following pages you will learn step by step with pictures how to thread leaves. You will learn the hook and the sprig technique. We will briefly describe how to thread flowers and what the loop technique is all about. The hook technique shown here can also be used to thread small, soft fruits (e.g. cranberries or little grapes).

Tips:

- The wire should be kept invisible as much as possible, because it does not look good.
- When you wire your material, be careful you don't damage the leaves or flowers. You can avoid this by supporting the leaf or the flower with your thumb and forefinger at the moment you perforate it. Patience and practice are the keywords!
- If you want to fold the wire with a nice, short angle, then use the flat side of a potato peeler to bend the wire around it.
- Choose the right size of wire. The size depends on the weight of the material that you want to wire. The thicker and heavier the material, the thicker the wire. For light material, e.g. leaves, berries and other light fruits or flowers, you can use 26-gauge corsage wire. For heavier flowers, e.g. roses, you will need 24-gauge wire. For really heavy materials, like pinecones or other heavy fruits, use 18-gauge or even 16-gauge wire.
- A common technique to finish the wiring of plant material is the splint method. Once you have perforated the material, you twist both ends of the plied wire as follows: one end follows the material's stem (the supporting end) and with the other end (the splint end) you secure the other two by turning it around a maximum three times. This basic technique is also useful to keep a bundle of conifer greenery together or to wire big leaves without a clear midrib, e.g. Hosta. First, you fold them together at the bottom of the leaf and from that point on you bind them together following the splint method.

1 | Threaded leaves

Lay the leaf upside down on the table with the twig towards you. Perforate the leaf a little above the middle, right next to the midrib and push the floral wire through the leaf. Let the wire come out of the leaf on the other side of the midrib. Gently pull the wire until the part that will serve as support leg is long enough (on the picture it is the part that comes out of the leaf on the left of the midrib). The length should be at least the distance from the perforation to the bottom end of the leaf plus the twig length.

Take the perforation area between your thumb and forefinger. With the other hand, take the floral wire and lay it downwards and parallel to the midrib. This way you will prevent the leaf from being damaged by the wire when you fold it.

 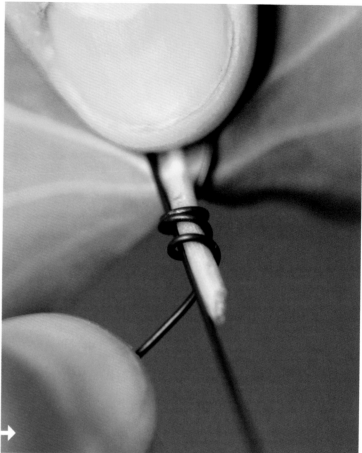

Move your thumb and forefinger from the perforation zone toward the leaf base and grasp it along with the two ends of the floral wire. Be careful that the support leg is parallel to the leaf twig. Fold the other end of the floral wire, the splint leg, with your other hand underneath the twig and the splint leg and twist it around them clockwise.

Tightly hold the leaf base and both legs of the floral wire. Twist the splint leg clockwise and in short turns around the twig and the support leg. Do this each time with one movement. Make sure that the floral wire does not cross itself on the twig. Instead, try to obtain a nice, spiral effect. Wrap the wire around the twig as far as possible and cut it with pliers at the desired length.

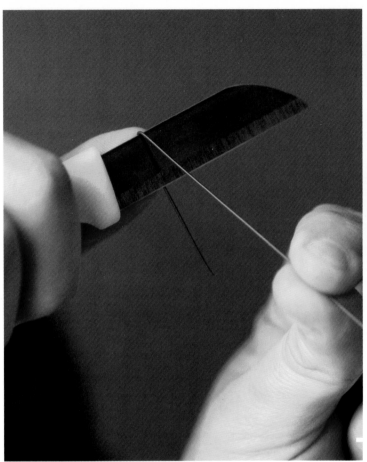 

2 | Hook technique

Fold the floral wire with your thumb, using the back of a potato peeler. This way you can obtain a nice, fine fold. Make sure the wire is not too long on one side.

Stick the other, long end of the wire into the heart of the flower. Push the wire totally through it and make sure it comes out on the bottom right next to the stem, underneath the flower head.

Pull the floral wire totally through the flower head. The hook should disappear nicely in the heart of the flower, until it is not visible anymore. Be careful not to pull too hard, otherwise you will destroy the flower.

Once the hook sits nicely in the flower heart, wrap the long end of the wire in wide movements around the flower stem so you cannot see that it is threaded. On the bottom you can either press the wire extra firmly against the stem or fold the end of the wire and insert it into the stem.

 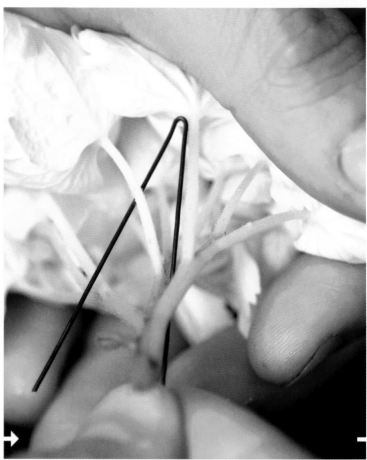

3 | Prig technique

The prig technique is applied to flowers with a branched, ball shaped head, e.g. Hydrangea macrophylla and Trachelium caeruleum. First thin out the ball shaped flower head to obtain several prigs.

Make a short hook of 5 to 10 cm in a 6 mm floral wire. The length of the hook depends on its use. Put the hook between the branches of the prig with both ends along the main branch.

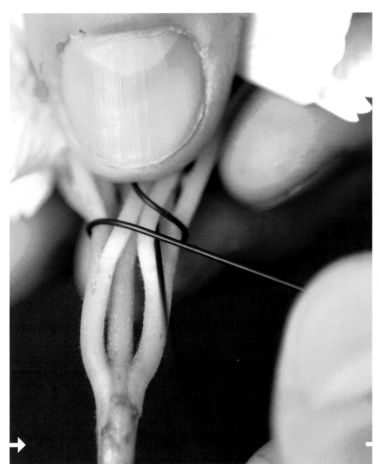

Carefully take the prig right behind the flower crown and make sure you also have the tip of the hook in your hands. Twist the splint leg with the other hand around the fine side branches and the other end of the wire, the support leg.

By binding the branches of the prig together as high as possible, the flower prig will be more compact. Finish with the splint method but try to wrap the main branch in the wire all the way up to the end. Cut the wire with pliers at the desired length.

4 | Threaded flowers

If you want to thread flowers, then this is the simplest method. Stick the end of the floral wire into the bottom of the flower head and twist the rest of the wire with a maximum of three big turns around the stem.

5 | Loop technique

Flowers that are placed in a vase, e.g. tulips, have to be supported in a different way. Here the loop technique is recommended. Make a loop around the stem, under the flower head. Then twist the floral wire with a maximum of three big turns around the stem over its entire length. You can make the loop as follows: bend the end of the wire around the jaws of the pliers until you obtain a more or less rounded shape. At the point where the curved part of the floral wire ends and the straight part starts, you give it a short 90° turn so the loop comes into a flat position, with underneath the long end of the floral wire at right angles. Open the loop a little, put the stem inside at the level of the flower bottom and close the loop up again.

Binding

1 to tie together, esp. with rope — **2** to tie up firmly — **3** to strengthen or decorate with a border of material — **4** to (cause to) stick together in a mass

According to Gudrun:

To fix or secure materials in order to form a larger whole

Possibilities:

• For ages the binding technique has been a popular way to bind bouquets. You can lay the bouquet flat on the table or keep it in your hands while making it, but in all cases you will have to bind the stems in order to keep them together. This is done with a soft material, meaning a material that will not damage the stems. The ideal alternatives are sisal, rope, raffia or floral bind wire.

• The binding technique can also be part of the arrangement itself. You can bind twigs into a flat whole or a mat, e.g. a placemat or a base to put an arrangement on. You can also make several mats or bundles and bind them together, shaping them into a basket.

• It is impossible to imagine flower arranging today without branches. Very often a base construction is made with carefully bound branches. Flowers can be clasped in between, and even placed in a small tube with water.

• You can keep things very easy and bind e.g. a grid of branches. The grid can be placed on top of a dish. This method is very practical because constructions like these can last for a very long time. You can freshen up the arrangement time after time by simply replacing the flowers. In any case, whether they are placed in a water tube or not, the flowers always have to be in water.

• The binding technique was used for the first garlands, festoons and wreaths. Today, it is still a very common technique. You can use winding wire to bind (bundles of) twigs or other materials around a solid rope or an existing or specially made form. This technique is very popular at Christmas because it allows the use of many materials that do not need any water at all.

Tips:

• If you are going to bind a mat made of branches, you can create nice shapes using an existing container, e.g. a vase or a pot.

• When binding thick or long sticks and branches, it is recommended to bind the material at two different points at the same time. This way you avoid the binding from warping.

• If you want to build a solid arrangement with branches, it is recommended to use dry branches. Fresh branches will continue shrinking for some time. As a result, the binding will get loose and the construction will become less stable.

• The ideal tool if you want to apply the binding technique is burnt winding wire, which becomes nicely weather-stained or rusty when you place the arrangement in the garden. Another practical tool is the above mentioned floral bind wire.

• It is not necessary to use much wire when binding. The most important is that you carefully tighten the wire, ideally with a pair of pliers.

• Your arrangement will look much nicer if you always bind following the same pattern or direction.

• It requires a considerable dose of patience to make good constructions. Sometimes you do not always see the results immediately. However, you will notice that the more you bind, the more solid your construction will become. You can be sure that your time and effort will be rewarded!

Step by step

> **Materials:**

Rosa, Euphorbia, Pulmonaria, Petasites (butterbur), Helleborus, Viburnum, Bergenia

1| First carefully prepare all the material. Take each individual piece of material, place one hand along the stem, starting at the top, and remove all the foliage (leaves, sprigs, prickles ...) that is under your hand. The point where the foliage is removed from, is called the binding point. It allows to easily tie up the bouquet. Once you have removed the foliage, you can lay all the flowers on the table, sorted by species.

2| Tie up your bouquet like a wheat sheaf. This means you have to wind the stems evenly slanting around the axis, just like a wheat sheaf. There are several techniques, but this one is ideal for beginners: take a firm branch of a certain species and keep it diagonally with the top inclined to the left. On the back, you now attach a firm branch of a

different species with the top inclined to the right. Both branches cross each other at the level of the so-called binding point. Therefore, this technique is simply called the 'front left/back right' technique.

Go along the line and each time pick only one stem. Hold the bundle or bouquet at the binding point and arrange every stem according to the 'front left/back right'. Turn the bouquet from time to time in your hand to avoid it becoming too flat and take care that the colours (just like the materials) are nicely distributed. At the top it should have the shape of a smooth ball, without any holes or elements sticking out. At the end you can include some additional foliage. This way the bouquet will look nicely balanced.

>>>

3| When all stems are included, you can tie up the bouquet at the level of the binding point. Take approximately three feet of rope or floral bind wire. Make a loop at the end and pull it over a firm stem on the outside of the bundle. Pull the loop up to the binding point and start winding the rope around the bundle. At the end the short end of the loop is attached to the long end.

4| Cut all stems at an angle and place the bouquet in a suitably-sized vase. Fill the vase with water up to the binding point.

Tips: To keep your bouquets beautiful for a longer time, it is recommended to add food to cut flowers in their vase water. It makes the flowers stronger and will give you hours of enjoyment. Change the water every two or three days and cut the stems on the bias. You may want to put the bouquet in a cooler place in the evening. Making small bouquets is less time-consuming than e.g. composing Biedermeiers, but they often have the same effect. Maybe a nice idea to decorate your table?

Tulip basket

Bind previously bleached maize rootstocks together with winding wire. Bind the stocks at two different points for a sturdier structure. Join both ends of the bound structure and place the structure around a plastic container. Fill all cavities with flat moss. Fill the container with short cut tulips in different colours.

34

Pinus basket

Remove needles from all Pinus branches. Take advantage of their flexibility by binding them into a half-ball while they are bent. Plant violets inside and fill with flat moss to finish.

Vase out of branches

Bind dried, straight branches into a mat
and wrap them around a glass vase. Attach
the same kind of branches on the inside.
In between, place Hippeastrum 'La Paz'
and bilberry Vaccinium myrtillus. Use quail
eggs to finish.

Trio of amusing winter vases

Grey shades are in, especially for winter arrangements. These amusing bouquets with sturdy material, including Eucalyptus, Eryngium, different safari materials and Viburnum tinus, were manually bound. The snow spray and the silver Christmas bauble create a festive atmosphere.

Nest of birch branches

Cut birch branches very short and tie them
up in bundles. Arrange the bundles around
the floral foam in the dish. Place a broken
ostrich egg in the middle of the dish. Stick
beautiful white and green turban buttercups
(Ranunculus inra 'Success Green') into the
wet floral foam. Finish the arrangement
with moss, quail eggs and wisps.

Wrapping

Possibilities:

- This technique is very practical to hide the auxiliary materials used, e.g. when you make a corsage, you will normally attach the materials to a metal wire. For aesthetic reasons the wire is wrapped in floral tape.
- You can use natural materials to wrap certain elements of your arrangement. This way, wrapping becomes one of the main techniques. Floral foam can be wrapped in Bergenia leaves, Macleaya, Lotus leaves, large sheets of flexible bark, etc. In between you can perfectly stick flowers into the floral foam or place them in the water tubes.
- The wrapping technique is also useful to wrap up moulds or frames. Therefore you will obviously need flexible materials: vines of all kinds of climbing plants, e.g. Hedera, silver-lace vine, honeysuckle, grapevine ... or stems of Vinca major, Gaura ...
- Another possibility is to use dried materials, such as pulp cane (which is available in a wide variety of colours) or artificial materials, e.g. plastic film, the inner tube of a bike tyre, etc.

Tips:

- If you are going to wrap auxiliary elements, make sure you choose the right materials: it is very important that you pick colours and styles that match the other materials used.
- Think about choosing a natural solution. E.g., if you are going to use plastic test tubes and you want to hide the plastic, you can wrap the tubes in evergreen leaves, like Hedera or Aspidistra.
- If you decide to wrap up certain parts of your arrangement, it is possible that you won't be able to provide the plants with water. In that case, you should choose plant material that can resist some time without water or material that remains beautiful once it is dry, e.g. grape vine leaves, butterbur, Macleaya leaves ... The drying of foliage material and flowers also depends on their maturity. Materials that are processed in fall have more chance of drying beautifully than others picked in spring.
- If you use flexible stems, take into account that vegetable materials shrink as they dry. It would not be the first time that a structure, wrapped in vines, completely loses stability after a couple of days!
  Sometimes it is possible to reduce the shrinking effect by adding some material to the wrapped structure. However, the ideal is to use materials that hardly change at all. We have obtained very good results with light green pulp cane and slim Vinca Major vines.

Step by step

> **Materials:**
aluminium thread, flexigrass, Delphinium, Convolvulus arvensis (field bindweed)

1| Fill the container with water. Bend the aluminium thread into a
pyramid shape.

2| Attach Delphiniums in between the thread.

3| I know the gardeners among you are not very fond of Convolvulus
arvensis, but if you remove the foliage, it is ideal for this arrangement. It is very flexible. Wrap it around the structure, combined with
flexible grass.

Spring cylinder

Wrap metal wire around a cylinder shape (e.g. a piece of PVC tube, Ø 10 cm) and wrap the cylinder in fresh green pulp cane. At the beginning the pulp cane tends to come loose. Keep on wrapping and you will notice that the structure becomes increasingly more solid. Attach glass tubes to each other with green binding wire. Place Fritillaria meleagris in the water-filled tubes.

Tulip bouquet

Cut willow branches (Salix) to the same length and arrange them around a glass vase. Use a rubber band to keep the branches in place. Arrange short parrot tulips on the inside. Hide the rubber band with a rope and wrap sea grass (Stipa tenacissima) around it. As additional decoration you can glue wisps and pieces of lapwing egg with a glue gun.

Tip: The arrangement will look even nicer if you place it on a dish.

Wrapped lotus leaves

Wrap dry lotus leaves (Nelumbo nucifera) in a trumpet shape and secure plastic tubes in the middle. Place the different leaves next to each other in a matching flowerpot. Place lilac roses in the water-filled tubes and finish with coral fern.

Pyramid of leaves

Stick long pieces of aluminium wire at different points in the pumpkin. Attach the pieces of wire to each other in such a way that you obtain a pyramid shape. Wrap the aluminium wire in green pulp cane. The pulp cane looks very natural. To make your arrangement sturdier, it is recommended to wrap a few pieces of aluminium wire around it. When the gaps become smaller due to the large quantity of wire, you can start filling the remaining gaps with autumn leaves.

Keep the autumn leaves in their position by wrapping pulp cane and aluminium wire around them. Glue small malus apples onto the autumn pyramid with a glue gun. It is also possible to wrap the pumpkin without piercing it. This way it will keep for much longer.

Fall cube

Fix a floral foam pin holder with adhesive onto a concrete clinker and put wet floral foam on top. Wrap the floral foam with flat moss and cover with the vines of the Virginia creeper (Parthenocissus). Finish off with bundles of Echinacea purpurea, unripe threaded grapes, a single rose and an amaranth shoot (Amaranthus), which you thread as well. Fill the holes with flat moss.

Pinning

According to the dictionary:

Mossing pin: **1** horse-shoe shaped wire with sharp ends that can be inserted into a material to secure another material

To pin: **1** to fasten or join with a pin or pins

According to Gudrun:

To secure green materials that keep well without water for some time or permanently (e.g. conifers, Hedera, bay laurel, etc.) onto a base of straw, polystyrene, floral foam, etc. by means of mossing pins

Possibilities:

- Mossing pins are used in techniques such as applications and sticking. You can use them to secure green materials onto the base. E.g. when you make an arrangement in a dish, you can fill some large areas with cushion moss and attach the moss to the base with pins. The classical Advent wreath is made following the same technique: little bundles of conifer green are fixed onto a straw wreath with pins.
- Mossing pins exist in different types and sizes. There are two types: the common mossing pins with a straight top and the patent mossing pins with a curved top. The shape of the latter allows better fixing of the material. You can also make your own mossing pins with pieces of floral wire. According to the material that you want to secure, you can use 0,6 mm to 1,2 mm or 1,5 mm floral wire.
- Common mossing pins are hard to find these days, except for a certain type, the so-called strawflower pins, and only in one size (5 mm large by 20 mm long). The name obviously refers to floral arranging with dry materials, but we still use them in the first place for leaf applications, e.g. for sphere-shaped arrangements where we attach fine Eucalyptus leaves to a polystyrene or grey floral foam sphere. The same thing can be done to cover other surfaces, e.g. Aspidistra elatior or Cordyline petiolaris leaves, cut into strips. You can also use little Laurus nobilis leaves.
- Wholesalers especially sell patent pins in different sizes (10 mm large; 30 mm – 80 mm long). There are also pins with a larger backside (17 mm), but they are not generally available. They are fairly sturdy pins that are very suitable to secure bigger materials, even onto hard surfaces such as straw wreaths. A classical example is the Advent wreath. But funeral wreaths and the like are often covered with diverse green materials, such as conifers, Prunus laurocerasus or Laurus nobilis leaves.

Tips:

- First wrap a plaster around your thumb. You can even put something hard underneath. This way you will avoid getting blisters.

51

Step by step

> **Materials:**
straw wreath, mossing pins, window tape, bay laurel (Laurus nobilis), box tree (Buxus sempervirens), hazel catkins (Corylus avellana)

1| Wrap the window tape around the straw wreath. When the wreath dries, the base — in this case the straw wreath — will be less visible if you first cover it with plastic window tape.

2| First cut all box tree branches, bay laurel branches and hazel catkins to the same length. Make bundles of them and secure them with a mossing pin to the straw wreath. Place the pinned bundles nicely arranged in a row, next to each other. For the next row, take bundles of green and secure them at a lower level, covering the previous row of pins.

Add a hazel catkin branch from time to time. Make sure that all bundles are equally thick. This way the wreath will have an even thickness. Arrange the end of the wreath under the point where you started. If you like, you can use slightly shorter bundles for the last row.
Use the same technique for Christmas wreaths. The end is often finished with a ribbon and a matching bow.

Autumn leaf as base

Finish the edges of an elongated floral foam dish with autumn leaves, which you stick in groups into the floral foam. By overlapping the groups you can easily hide the mossing pins. Stick short-stemmed roses (Rosa) on top. Clasp some autumn leaves in between and decorate with pink pepper balls and twigs of unripe dates.

Autumn stump

Cover a big polystyrene wreath with dry
autumn leaves. Use pins to secure them.
Attach a plastic dish with wet floral foam
to the wreath. The floral foam has to be
nicely cut and rounded off. Stick different
types of roses in the half sphere and mix
them with small, red harvest apples and
wild chestnuts on a stick. Fill the small
gap with balls of autumn leaves. A hollow
stump serves as stand.

Tulip wreath in basket

This simple arrangement with tulips and moss is ready in no time and fills your house with a spring-like atmosphere. The base of the arrangement is a wreath. Secure ball moss or cushion moss to the wet floral foam wreath with mossing pins. Intersperse with small groups of very short cut tulips and threaded ivy berries (Hedera helix) and bilberries. The wreath will look really stunning if you put it in a basket or bowl.

Lighted star

Cut a square piece of polystyrene and put it on small trunks with nails ('floating' arrangements always look very elegant). Cover the polystyrene with flat moss with mossing pins. Arrange the Christmas lights in between the moss and secure it with mossing pins. Leave a gap in the middle for the cranberries. You can prick them individually with a small, wooden stick if you like. The cranberries can come a little higher in the middle than on the sides. Salix branches give the star even more shape. Finish with coral fern.

Pinned Christmas tree

Cut a thick polystyrene plate (4 cm thick) into a pyramid shape. Start at the bottom with pieces of silver fir (Abies) pinned next to each other. The second row should nicely overlap the first one. When you get to the top of the tree, cover the polystyrene with smaller pieces of silver fir. Fix them with a glue gun. The decoration is consciously kept very austere. The tree is only covered with a generous quantity of exotic fruits and unripe dates, painted with gold spray and fixed with glue.

Application

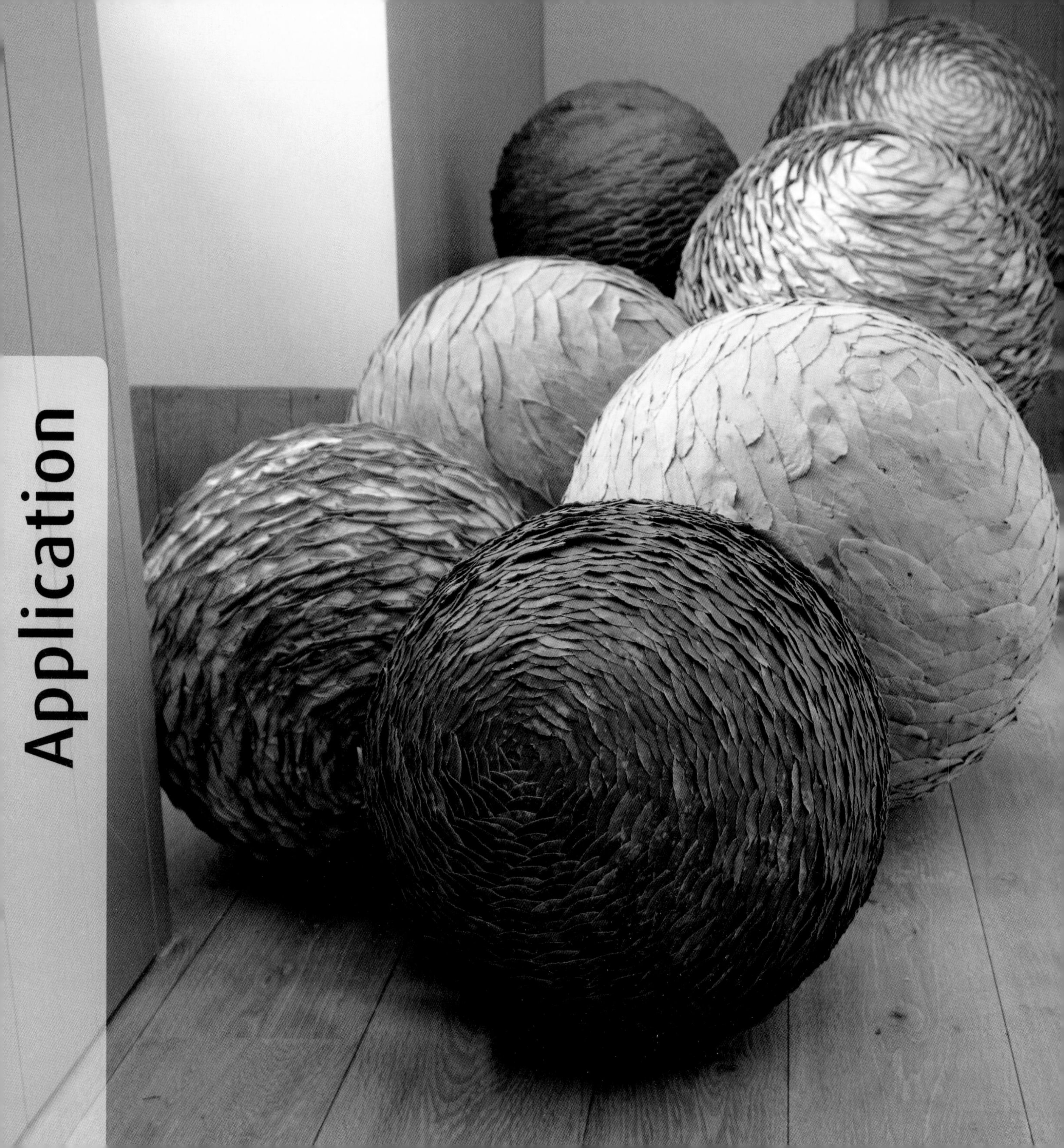

According to the dictionary:

1 the act of putting something to use — **2** a particular practical use — **3** the putting of one thing onto another — **4** careful and continuous attention or effort — **5** (the act of making) a request

According to Gudrun:

For applications, apart from the plant material you need a clear surface that will serve as the base of your arrangement. The most common plant material used here is foliage. Therefore we often speak of leaf application. It is considered here as a separate technique because over the past few years it has become quite popular.

An application implies that you attach the plant material to the surface using some additional aid and applying a secondary technique, e.g. clamps (clasping technique), cold glue (glueing technique), pins (sticking technique) ...

Possibilities:

- The surface can be a piece of wood, polystyrene, floral foam ... The aids you use to attach the plant material depend on both the surface and the plant material. E.g., if you want to make a wooden frame with fresh leaves, you will have to glue the leaves with cold glue. If you want to cover the same frame with pieces of Pinus bark, you should use a glue gun.
- If you work with polystyrene or grey floral foam balls, pyramids or plates, pins and greening pins are the best methods to attach elements. I often prefer greening pins. As they have two ends, the leaf cannot turn around the axis and remains better in place than if you use a common pin (see also tips for combinations of aids in applications).
- An application can be part of an arrangement, e.g. a ball with an application, partly filled with fine elements.

Tips:

- When you apply the leaves, these should overlap each other. The part perforated to attach the leaf is covered by the following leaf. This way you not only obtain very regular joints, but you also avoid the surface becoming visible once the plant material starts to dry and shrink.
- If you want to maintain a regular structure in your application, e.g. using elements that overlap each other, try to keep the same distance between the different elements. If the first row of application is very tight and the elements in the next rows are spread out, the result will look untidy.
- Sometimes the leaves of the plant material have a different colour and/or texture on each side. You can create a very decorative effect by working in different, alternate layers: in the first row you place the leaves in one position, in the next row you place them upside-down. Examples of such plants are Elaeagnus x ebbingei or Viburnum davidii.
- You will often need to combine different aids. You can make the joints in leaf applications even more beautiful if you stick the leaves that you are placing onto the overlapping part of the leaves in the previous row, e.g. with cold glue. This way you avoid showing the greening pins when the leaves begin to curl and when they start to dry up.
- As the plant material tends to shrink during the drying process, it is recommended to make applications out of 'ripened' material. Therefore, the plants that you find in autumn and winter are ideal. Plant materials of Mediterranean origin (e.g. Eucalyptus) are an excellent alternative.

Step by step

> **Materials:**
styrofoam ball, strawflower pins (= small mossing pins), Elaeagnus leaves, cold glue

1| Pin an Elaeagnus leaf (use the bottom side of the leaf) on the edge. Arrange different kinds of elongated leaves around it. Carefully pin the edges of the leaf to avoid curling when it dries. The distance between the leaves must always be the same. This is applicable to the leaves that are placed next to each other and to the ones that overlap each other.

2| Continue until the polystyrene is completely covered. Near the end you may not be able to hide all the last mossing pins.

3| Finish the sphere by fixing one or more leaves with cold glue on top of the last leaves.

Tip: When you have finished, tightly pull a nylon stocking over the sphere. Within a few days you will notice that the leaves have perfectly adapted to the shape of the sphere. Big spheres can be wrapped in elastic bandage.

Bottom of the sphere (finished off with glued leaves)

A container to use time after time

Cut several blocks of dry green floral foam into the desired shape and attach them to each other with wooden sticks. Spoon out a piece of foam so you can lay a plastic film and some wet floral foam on top of the structure. On the dry part, attach Viburnum leaves. Cover the edge with abele. Prick different kinds of short rose stems into the wet floral foam.

Tip: Choose leaves that dry nicely. This arrangement can take quite a long time, but you can use it again forever: just change the plant material. It is definitely worth the effort.

Cordyline as base

The base is composed of insulation plates, cut out with a snappy knife and attached to each other with screws. You can create an endless variety of shapes with this insulation material. Cover the plates with Cordyline leaves, cut into strips and secured with flat, thick, short nails. Place a small dish with wet floral foam on top. Cut several burgundy roses short and arrange them next to each other. Use Scottish red moss and coral fern to finish.

Glueing

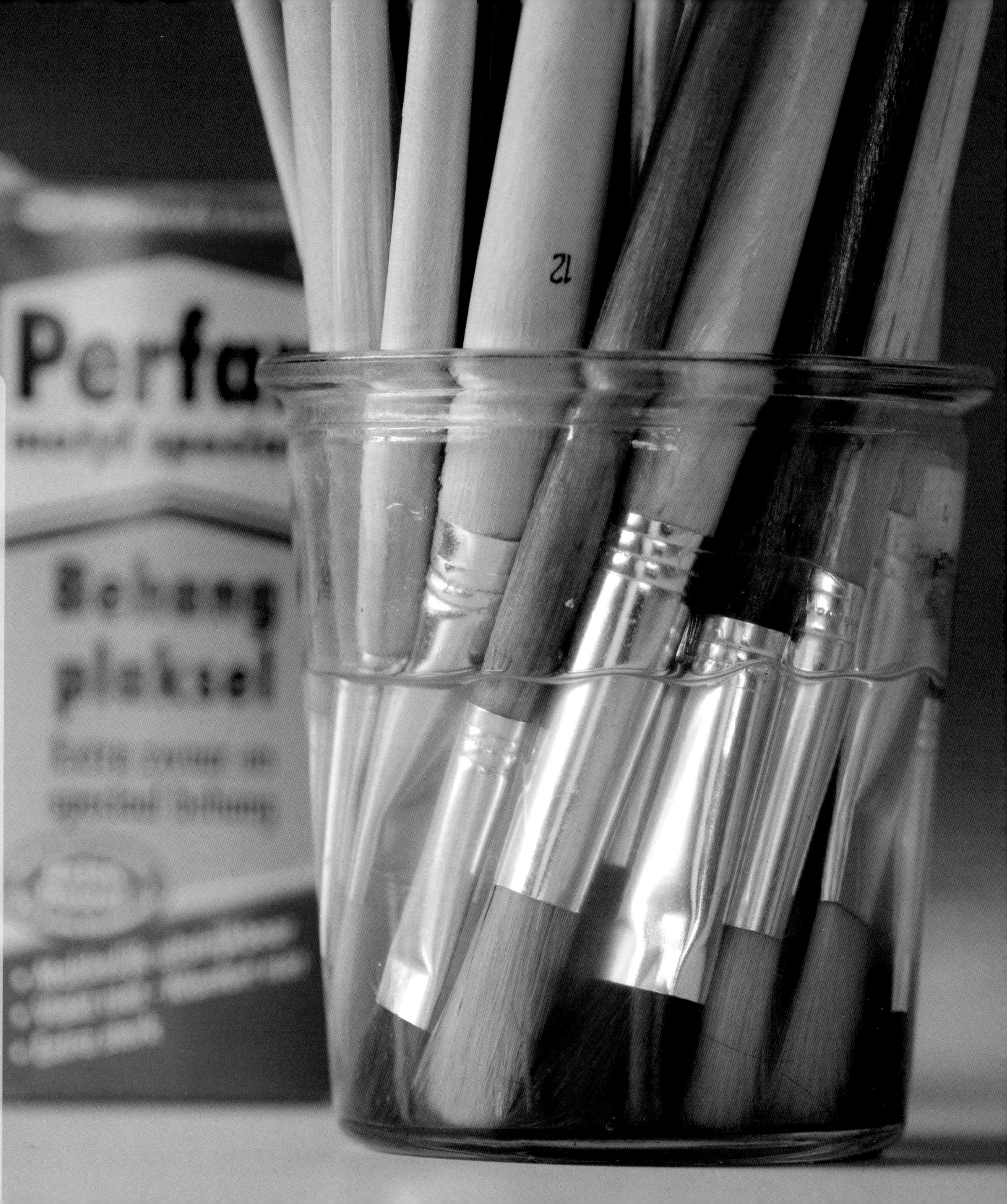

Possibilities:

• When you read old books on flower arranging, you will notice that there is little or almost nothing said about glueing. If you find something about it at all, it will usually be descriptions of glueing as an auxiliary element and not that much about it as a technique.

Although the discussion is still open, we opt for glueing as a technique, because it plays an important role in contemporary flower arranging and offers a wide range of application possibilities. Florists use many kinds of glue. At the beginning, it was simply used to fix floral foam into the dish or container. Later the glue gun appeared. But the great breakthrough was caused by the introduction of cold glue. Today, more and more different glueing products, like glue spray and even wallpaper paste are being used in flower arrangements.

Tips:

• Cold glue: if you are going to work with delicate, fresh materials (leaves, flowers, berries, etc.) and you want to avoid damaging the plant material with the glue, then you must use cold glue. Although working with this kind of glue may be a hassle, it is vital for the flower arrangement. Important tip: apply some glue and wait at least one minute before mounting the material.

• Glue gun: if you want to stick heavier, solid or dead materials (cinnamon sticks, nuts and other dried fruits, and even Malus apples) a glue gun is recommended. Make sure the material is dry. Only use high quality glue sticks and be careful not to burn yourself. The base of your arrangement is very important. E.g. it is not a good idea to use hot glue on polystyrene because in many cases it tends to melt. Try wrapping the polystyrene in fabric, ribbon, etc. In other words: prepare a base that is easy to glue on.

• The use of glue spray is usually limited to fixing powder sugar or gold glitter on Christmas greenery. But today glue spray is also used as a glueing technique to give shape to green arrangements. The material that you use to form a certain sculpture, should be dry and light (e.g. leaves, pine needles). Use a sufficiently powerful glue spray. It is a good idea to test the glue before you apply it. Avoid applying glue spray on flowers!

• Wallpaper paste exists in many different forms. Solid wallpaper paste is recommended if you want stick leaves, e.g. abele, onto polystyrene, wood, etc. in a very user-friendly way. Common wallpaper paste is suitable to attach natural elements to existing or self-made structures. Wallpaper paste has the advantage that it sticks to many different surfaces.

• Less common but worth mentioning are the powerful glues that we use to glue floors or tiles. They can be a solution when you want to secure large elements, such as stones, thick branches, etc.

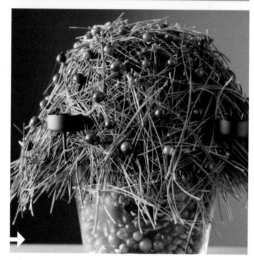

Step by step

> **Materials:**
cranberries (Vaccinium macrocarpon), pineapples, Pinus palustris, Schinus (red pepper balls)

1| Mix cranberries and pine apples in a glass vase. Clasp an floral foam cake dummy in a plastic dish. On top of the vase place a tea light candle holder.

2| Place the plastic dish with floral foam on top of the glass vase. Pin long pine needles (e.g. Pinus palustris) in bundles around the floral foam cake dummy. You will need this layer as the base for the next layers.

3| Spray glue on the loose pine needles and arrange them on the base in several layers. It is recommended to work in thin layers. Create a nice, round shape. If you give the glue some time to dry a little, it will stick better.

4| Glue the cranberries on the pine needles with a glue gun.

5| Strew some red pepper balls over the arrangement.

Square with shells

With the glue gun, glue long razor shells (Solen marginatus) around the square polystyrene. Place a wet floral foam plate on the inside and stick Eryngium 'Sirius Q Star' onto it.

Birch vase

For this arrangement I chose a vase with a crack. By sticking pieces of birch with a glue gun, the vase was ready to be used again! Place a dish with wet floral foam in the vase. Fill it with bilberry (Vaccinium myrtillus) and plastic tubes. Arrange flowers like Gerbera 'Torina' and Ranunculus 'Elegance Hot Pink'. Use Iceland moss (Cetratia islandica) to decorate the edges.

Cinnamon sticks

With a glue gun, glue small cinnamon sticks next to each other around a bent frame. Attach a small piece of floral foam on top and prick Chrysanthemums, use two different colours close to each other.

Eucalyptus basket

Glue pieces of Eucalyptus bark onto an old basket with a glue gun. Plant Meulenbeckia on the inside. Stick glass tubes with Gloriosa flowers between the Meulenbeckia. Curl scarlett runners and tie them up. Secure them between the plants and the flowers with long mossing pins.

Birch wreath

Cover a floral foam wreath on the in- and outside with pieces of birch bark (that reach higher than the floral foam) with a glue gun. Cut the white cluster roses short and stick them nicely spread in the floral foam. Fill the gap with Icelandic moss. Use birch bark pearls and stars to decorate.

Tip: Another attractive idea is to lay little birch bark stars over the wreath and put a candle in the middle.

Christmas spheres for orchid

Cut a notch on the top of the polystyrene ball. Secure the ball with anchor tape. Fix big, beautiful pieces of dry tree bark on the sphere with a glue gun. Fill the gaps between the pieces of bark with small wads of cotton wool. Poor melted paraffin over the sphere. Clasp a brick of wet floral foam in the gap in the polystyrene. Fill it with Dendrobium and a branch of unripe blue dates. Hide the floral foam under flat green moss.

Drift wood wreath

This wreath is inspired by drift wood from the Breton coast. Fix the pieces of wood on a straw wreath with a glue gun. Fill the gap with dry autumn leaves.

Bark dish with Lysianthus

Cut a few centimeters from the upper edge of a half polystyrene sphere. This way you create a shape that looks more like a dish than like a half sphere. With a glue gun, glue big, dry pieces of tree bark on the in- and outside. Fill the holes with flat moss. Place a small water dish in the middle. Put a small half floral foam sphere in the dish and cover it with Lysianthus.

Cinnamon wreath

Cover a floral foam wreath with cinnamon sticks, using glue. On top you can attach alternately groups of Chrysanthemum 'Santini Basketarini' and Limquats (small limes) and ball moss.

Shaping & Modelling

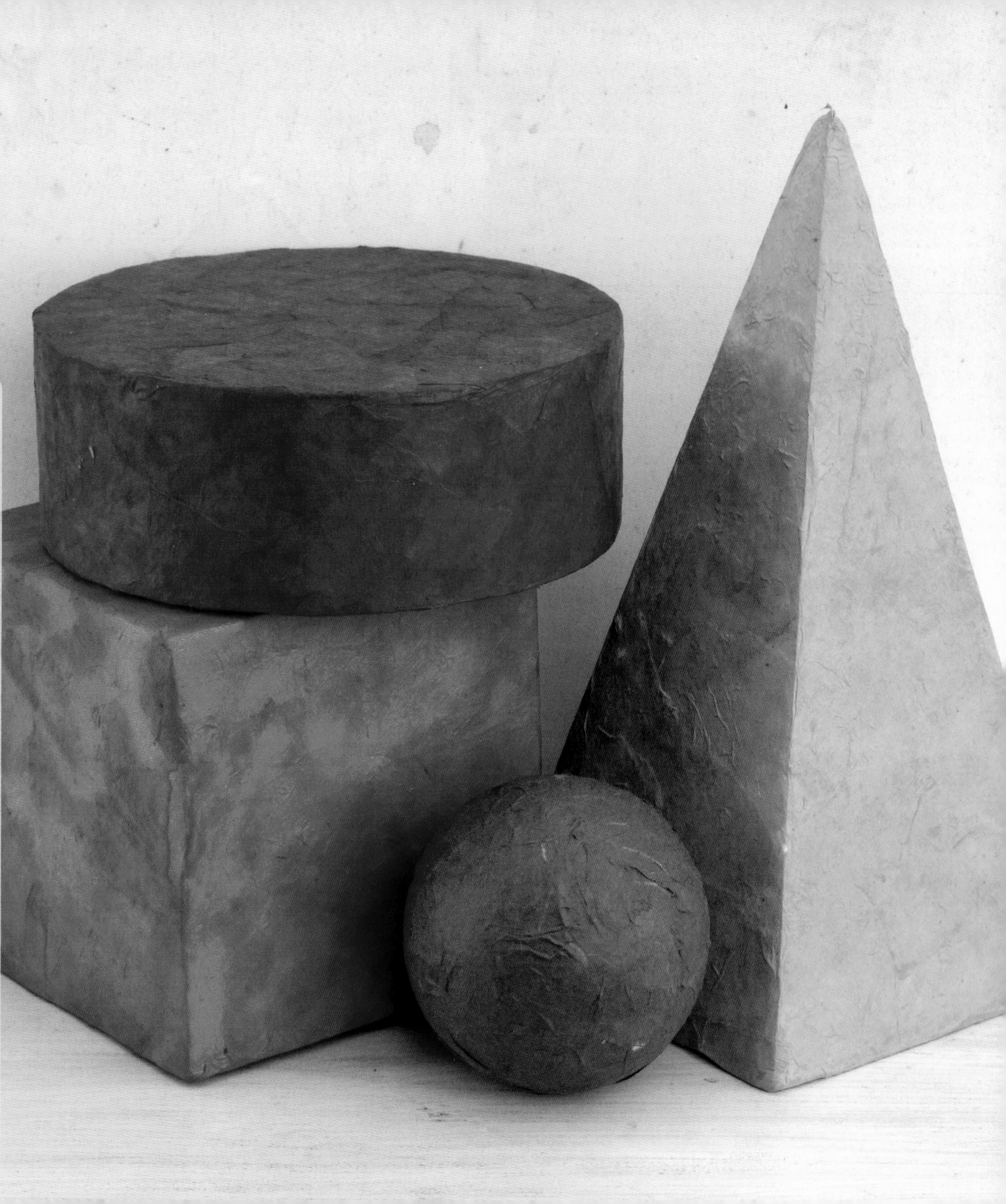

According to the dictionary:

To shape: **1** to make or form, esp. to give a particular shape or form to

To model: **1** to shape (a soft or kneadable substance) into an article

According to Gudrun:

When we use the words shaping and modelling, we mean the creation of a self-made structure with a certain shape. With this technique you can let your creativity go. Especially with plastic materials, you can do a thousand things.

Possibilities:

- In flower arranging there is a growing tendency to use this technique, because it allows endless variety. The biggest advantage is that you can create something unique that you will not see anywhere else.
- You have to distinguish between covering existing forms or creating your own without using an existing base.
- One of the most common techniques is cutting floral foam into the desired shape. You can make big structures combining different blocks, which you attach to each other with sticks. You can also use a big floral foam block (deco block).
- The use of clay is a technique that was very popular in the past to secure plant materials. You can also use clay to model a certain form and attach the flowers to it afterwards. Another possibility is to cover an existing form (in polystyrene or other material) with plant material, e.g. with moss, and to apply a clay layer. The clay will crack during the drying process, creating a very special effect.
- You can cover an existing or self-made form with papier-mâché. Use pieces of paper or other materials, such as natural fibres, wisps, etc. treated with wallpaper paste. They are very suitable for this technique and give a nice effect.
- Extra fast plaster, coloured or not, gives a quick and surprising result. You can use it on different hard, dry materials (polystyrene, wood, etc.).
- Materials drenched in melted candle-wax give very surprising results. You can also use candle-wax to make an original container.
- Polystyrene can be an ideal base to cover with other materials. You can cut the polystyrene, make it smaller or scrape the bottom out of a half-ball.
- Fine materials such as pine needles, eggshells, etc. can be glued together with a strong spray glue. If you work very carefully and build the structure layer by layer, you can create a very original, surprising container.

Tips:

- The best way to shape floral foam is using another piece of floral foam. It is best to do this when the foam is dry. When it is wet, you will make a mess and it will be a highly laborious job.
- You can apply the papier-mâché technique on any plastic form. Cover the plastic with liquid glycerine before you put the wallpaper paste on.
- Self-made forms sometimes have the disadvantage that they are not water-proof. The solution is to place a smaller, plastic container inside your self-made container.
- Re-use the forms that you have made in the past. You can give them a totally new look by adding new materials.

Step by step

> **Materials:**

floral foam, big knife, small knife, plastic tubes, black lichen, sewing pins, Anemone coronaria

1| Roughly cut the floral foam bricks with a big knife. Then touch them up with a small knife and finish by smoothing them with another floral foam brick until you obtain the perfect shape. Keep both floral foam bricks together with wooden sticks. Slightly hollow the top of the base with a teaspoon.

2| Cover the bottom of the floral foam with lichen. The easiest way to do it is with sewing pins.

3| Place plastic tubes in the hollowed out top. Finish the arrangement with Anemone coronaria to complete the concept.

Arch with green materials

Before you start smoothing the floral foam into an arch shape, it is recommended to make and work on a paper mould. Cover the outside of the arch with ninebark leaves (Physocarpus opulifolius). Use small mossing pins to fix them. Attach the different bricks to each other with wooden sticks. Place a dish with wet floral foam on top. Fill it with Physocarpus berries, Cotinus and Astrantia major 'Ruby Red' filaments and threaded unripe grapes. The arrangement looks more elegant if you place it on a stand, in this case square candles.

Fragile

Tear wrapping paper (similar to butter paper) into small pieces. Heat candle-wax until it is completely melted and submerge the paper strips one by one in the candle-wax. Stick them immediately on the polystyrene ball because it dries quickly. Once dry, it looses its glueing effect. Then put a small piece of wet floral foam into the ball and fill with white Dianthus barbatus.

Tip: Use handmade paper to get another beautiful result.

Gerbera bowl

Cut a piece of polystyrene from the ball. The hole should be big enough to attach a floral foam wreath. Cut off a small slice of polystyrene on the bottom to give the ball a solid base. Mix Joint filler with some water and paint. Cover the polystyrene ball with this mixture. Fill the wet floral foam wreath with Gerberas in a monotonous colour. Add Gerbera leaves to the Joint filler before it is completely dry. When the Joint filler dries, the flowers will be fixed.

Strawberries as main material

Fold chicken wire in two and fill it with sea grass (Stipa tenacissima). This way, you obtain a self-made basket. Use flat moss to fill the basket on the inside and lay strawberries on top. Finish the edge with Sempervivum and attach it to the chicken wire basket with wooden sticks.

Tip: The fruit stays fresh for longer if you don't perforate it.

Muscari in clay

Cover a polystyrene half-ball with clay. Place a Muscari plant inside the ball and finish with flat moss.

Curved paper structure

Cut a band of approximately 8 cm from a big polystyrene half sphere. Now cut this disk in two and attach both pieces into a playful shape. Cover them with hand-made paper and wallpaper paste. Fill the gap with wet floral foam in plastic. The structure and the floral foam should form a harmonious whole. Stick small Cymbidiums in the floral foam. Fill the gaps with pieces of red cabbage leaves and coal. These two materials combine very well with each other and especially with the colours of the Cymbidiums.

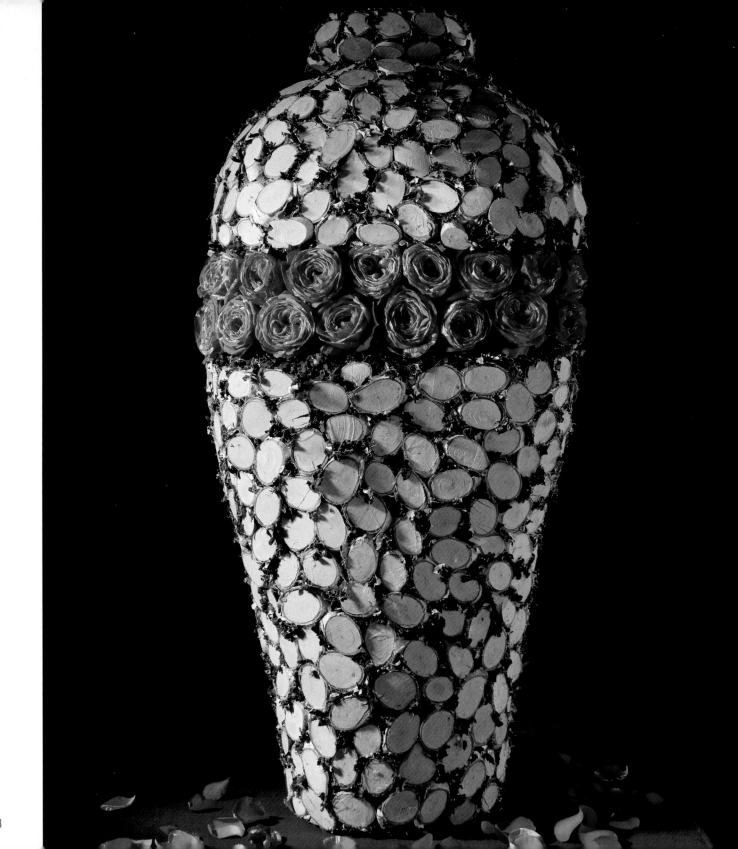

Lichen vase

Cut and smoothe a vase from a big piece of floral foam: quite a big task, but worth a try. Cover the floral foam with
the underside of the lichen. Attach a piece of plastic between lid and bottom using mossing pins and place a
wet piece of floral foam on top. Fix the lid to the bottom with long wooden skewers. Finish off with short stems
of roses (Rosa ranunculus).

Weaving & branding

According to the dictionary:

Braid: **1** to twist together several lengths of a flexible material (e.g. thread) to form one rope like length.

Weave: **1** to form threads into material by drawing one thread at a time under and over a set of longer threads, to form by twisting parts together

According to Gudrun:

Braiding is a structured way of twisting flexible vegetable materials (e.g. twines, lines, tendrils, vines, grass ...). Weaving is a form of twisting certain flexible materials into a horizontal or vertical lattice, creating one consistent whole, usually a surface.

Possibilities:

- Braiding can be part of an arrangement. E.g. you can make a vine wreath and attach other materials onto it, or a woven cylinder that can give shape to a bouquet.
- My favourite time of the year to braid is spring. Most branches do not have any leaves yet and they are still very flexible. Braided arrangements last a lot longer than most cut flowers, but it is possible to use the same base several times and just change the flowers from time to time.
- You can also braid vegetable materials with other flexible materials, e.g. lead strips, aluminium thread, textiles ...
- Braiding and weaving using an existing base is another possibility, e.g. a metal grid, a wooden frame with wire mesh, welded metal bars, etc. It works faster and comes in very handy.
- You can use wet floral foam in a container as the base of your braiding. Wet floral foam is more solid than when it is dry, especially when you want to prick dry branches into it. Place the straight branches into the wet floral foam and braid in a horizontal direction. Use different patterns and materials: braid a border with grass, then use twigs and then grass again.

Tips:

- Check the flexibility of the branches before you start. Obviously dry material is less suitable for braiding. You can first bend the material a little bit by holding it firmly (this way you warm the branch) and making it more flexible by twisting it with short movements.
- If you have been pruning in fall and you want to wait a few weeks before you braid that beautiful Christmas wreath, then leave the vines and branches outside to keep them flexible.
- You can also (re)use dry twigs by placing them in water before use. This will give them their flexibility back.
- If you are working with flexible branches or vines, first remove all foliage and side twigs. This will make the braiding easier. Besides, leaves on the branches may create a messy look.
- If you use the braiding as the base of your arrangement (branch wreath), then it is important that the construction remains solid even after it has dried. Some materials shrink up to 50% or more of their volume when dry. Take this into account.
- Sometimes metal wire can be very handy to attach the branches to each other or as extra security when they are dry. But you will discover that the more you braid, the more solid your constructions will become and the less wire you will need!
- Material tip: most climbers have very flexible stems, e.g. Lonicera (honeysuckle), Wisteria (blue rain), Hedera (ivy), Parthenocisus (grape vine) ... but also the Convolvulus (bindweed). Typha angustifolia is also a very rewarding material for braiding work. You can find it in any flower shop.

Step by step

> **Materials:**
floral foam, container, pulp cane, Typha leaf, orchid leaf, plastic tubes, bleached Cobra leaf

1| Pack the container completely with wet floral foam up to the edges. Cut the floral foam to the height of the container. Stick pulp cane in the floral foam. Place it vertically and at equal distances. Braid Typha leaf in between the pulp cane.

2| Arrange a Cobra leaf in the braided structure. The Typha will shrink but thanks to the leaf, even then the arrangement will still be beautiful.

3| Place the plastic tube in the wet floral foam and put the orchid in the tube. Attach the orchid roots and leaf on the outside. You can use wooden sticks to attach them. Use Iceland moss (Cetratia islandica) to finish.

Woven flower container

Fill the container to the top with floral foam. Stick the thicker willow branches (Salix) vertically into the floral foam, spreading them equally. Weave supple twigs in between. Do not weave all the way round but only halfway. Do the same thing on the other side. Bind the ends together with a supple twig. Fill the centre with roses and willow catkins. Finish the arrangement with green pepper balls and Icelandic moss.

Woven base structure

The two concrete grids are welded onto an iron plate. The concrete wire is wrapped in floral tape. Weave wheat stems in groups through the grid. Place a small floral foam dish and fill with very short Eustoma 'Wonder el bro' and cut wheat. Eustoma 'Wonder el bro' looks gorgeous here because there is an enormous quantity of flowers on each branch.

According to the dictionary:

1 to hold firmly and tightly, — **2** to fix, tighten or squeeze something into or between something else by exerting pressure or by means of a clasp, buckle, etc.

According to Gudrun:

Clasping is a technique that consists of fixing or securing vegetable material by means of another material.

Possibilities:

The clasping technique is a fairly recent technique in European flower arranging. In Japanese ikebana it has existed for much longer. An example is the kubari method, using pieces of kubari (forked twigs) to secure other branches, flowers, leaves, etc. In the past we used clips mainly as a technique for the benefit of flower arranging. Over the past few years it has become a real trend to use the construction made with clasping and stretching techniques as an ornamental element on its own.

As a base material branches are very common, but we can also use other vegetable or even non-vegetable material to build the clasped construction.

Tips:

- The shape of the dish or container that you use is very important. Pots and dishes with a turned-in edge are most suitable when you want to use the clasping technique. The compressed wood tends to unfold but when it is obstructed by some obstacle, it becomes fixed really well .
- Flexible materials, e.g. branches and vines, are ideal for clasping. The main idea is that the material is strong but at the same time flexible.
- Sometimes the branches or twigs you use to clasp will not stay in place properly. You can make the construction sturdier by binding those branches and twigs at certain key points.
- Take into account that if you use humid material, it will shrink once it is dry. The dry material becomes loose, which is bad for the construction's sturdiness. Try using non-vegetable material to apply the clasping technique, e.g. chicken wire, metal grids, wooden or metal frames with an iron wire web tightened from side to side …
- The clasping technique is ideal for nice spring arrangements. In spring most flowers don't keep well for long, whereas the construction can last much longer. As the flowers are easy to replace, you can enjoy your arrangement for a very long time.
- Pure clasping techniques principally don't involve any binding or sticking. But just like in the culinary world, where the combination of different techniques has been the base of surprising fusion cooking, the combination of clasping and other techniques can produce very nice and innovative results. E.g. take a low container, filled to the top with floral foam and randomly arrange pieces of bark. In between the bark, you can clasp all kinds of vegetable material. If this material needs water, e.g. if you use flowers, you already have the soil needed because you can stick the flowers into the floral foam.

Step by step

> **Materials:**
big dish, ivy vines (Hedera), willow catkins (Salix), ball moss, Icelandic poppy (Papaver nudicaule) and Virginia creeper (Parthenocissus)

1| Braid the Virginia creeper into compact wickerwork. First remove all foliage and braid the branches while they are still flexible. Weave in a few ivy vines across the Virginia creeper.

2| Arrange the willow catkins vertically by clasping them in the wickerwork. The top of the branch has to stand upright if you want to obtain a tight branch structure.

3| Cut the Icelandic poppies at an angle and place them vertically in between the wickerwork and next to the willow catkins. Place the shortest stems on the outside.

Tip: Icelandic poppy is one of the few flowers that are scalded in the flower shop. If you cut the stem shorter, then it is best to scald it again.

Bent arrangement with Pinus

Remove all the needles from the Pinus branches, bend them slightly and arrange them in a dish. When you start making the structure it is recommended to secure a few branches with a piece of metal wire. Arrange the Christmas balls on the bottom of the dish. Place Zantedeschia 'Scharzwalder' in water-filled tubes and arrange them between the Pinus branches with a piece of binding wire. Fix the burgundy pomegranates between the branches. Use coral fern to finish.

Arrangement
with lilies

Hang Catalpa beanpods randomly
over the edge of a high glass vase.
Remove the excess foliage from the
Lilium 'Longiflorum White Europe' and
cut the stems at an angle. The lilies
should reach out a little above the
Catalpa beanpods.

Linear arrangement

For a floating effect, place a small glass pot in a glass dish and lay a big, square deco plate on top of it. The little pot will no longer be visible once the deco plate is on it. Attach the wheat (Triticum), Asclepias and Allium stems to the deco plate. Try to maintain the tight, square shape.

Colourful contrast

Stretch coloured elastic band over a flat dish filled with water. Arrange Gloriosa flowers in between in a harmonised way.

Helleborus arrangement

Use Joint filler to attach the vegetable gourd (Luffa acutangula) to the dish. Prick small water-filled glass tubes and Helleborus in the Luffa. Sprinkle the bottom of the dish with sand and pink pepper berries, matching the colour of the flowers.

Square arrangement for garden table

Prick the stem of the common butterbur (Petasites hybridus) in the floral foam. Make the leaf balls and secure the balls with greening pins. Bind elder branches (Sambucus nigra) into a grid with binding wire. Prick Sempervivum on a stick. Secure Rosa 'Peppermint' between the twigs. Thread Hypericum berries on steel grass and bend them between the twig structure.

Pulp cane flower container

Fill a zinc dish with coal and water. Form a circle with the pulp cane ribbon and secure it with staples. Attach the circles to each other with staples and lay them on the dish. Cut mini Gerberas short and at an angle. Clasp them into the circles and in between the coal.

Magnolia spring arrangement

Arrange very thin slices of bark shavings in a long dish. Prick tubes in between and fill them with Magnolia and flowering sprigs. You can nicely finish the arrangement with Iceland moss (Cetratia islandica).

Tip: We covered the dish, which we found too white, with dark polishing wax.

Wooden bowl with Muehlenbeckia

Fill a wooden bowl with Muehlenbeckia plants. Arrange glass tubes in between the Muehlenbeckias and fill the tubes with Helleborus and Muscari.

Stringing

According to the dictionary:
1 to put together or with others onto a thread, so as to form a string — **2** to put one or more strings on (a musical instrument)

According to Gudrun:
To connect vegetable materials that can hold for a certain time without water on a thread, cord or string. The goal is to create a green decoration chain.

Possibilities:

- The stringing technique is often used to make garlands and wreaths. Thanks to the flexibility of the material used it is possible to create movement in the string work. But it can also be used to pile up different materials. Both techniques are often founded on the same base, namely the repeated piercing or perforating decorative materials to produce a series or chain. However, it is not absolutely necessary to perforate the materials to pile them up. You can also do it within a solid structure where the green material cannot slide, e.g. a glass container, a wooden rack ...
- Stringing can be used as main technique but also as part of an arrangement. You can string different materials together and wind them like string around a vase, dish or other containers that you use as the base of your arrangement or bouquet.
- Some fine, fragile materials are not suitable for stringing. However, you can attach them afterwards, e.g. with a glue gun or by sticking materials on a wire or a stick.
- Autumn is the ideal time for stringing because the materials have become sufficiently resistant to keep well for a while without water or to dry beautifully in a natural way.

Tips:

- The ideal stringing tool is aluminium wire. If you choose a size that is not too thick, the garland or string will be flexible so you can move and turn it as you please. Alternatives are pulp cane and Flexigrass.
- Do not use humid materials, otherwise you may get fungus.
- You can also use the stringing technique to join big, not dentate leaves, e.g. Japanese creeper (Parthenocissus tricuspidata), London plane tree (Platanus acerifolia), Wild chestnut (Aesculus hippocastanum), etc.
- The art of stringing consists of joining the leaves (which are often different sizes) in such a way that they look identical. You will have to fold some leaves in to, others in three and leave other unfolded in order to keep the same width all the time.
- This technique is great to make beautiful wreaths, garlands and festoons. You can use autumn leaves and adapt the decoration according to the occasion. E.g. at Christmas you can use cranberries, in autumn chestnut shells and rose hips are very appropriate.
- Make strings with hearts to decorate door handles or cupboard keys. The effect is surprising!
- The stringing technique is fun to try out with children: quick and beautiful results with minimal resources.
- Have you ever thought of making a necklace with the stringing technique? One of the best materials to make a necklace is the gum-tree or Eucalyptus (Eucalyptus perriniana, E. cinerea and E. pulverulenta. The first two are winter-hardy to -4°C).

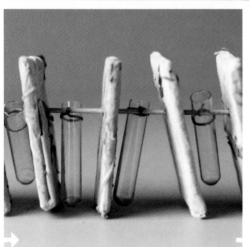

Step by step

> **Materials:**
metal spear, short glass tubes, decorative binding wire, a nail, plume poppy leaf (Macleaya), cornflower (Centaurea), cardboard moulds, floral cold glue

1| Cover the previously cut to size cardboard with the Macleaya leaf. Glue the leaf with floral cold glue. Put a lot of glue on the edges of the cardboard and wait a few seconds before attaching the leaf. This way, it will stick better. The ideal is to leave these coated forms drying under weights for a few days.

2| Perforate the coated forms with a nail. Make sure to perforate them all at the same point. Attach them to the spear, alternating with the water tubes. Attach the tubes using decorative binding wire.

3| Fill the tubes with water and place the short cut cornflowers in them.

Tip: This is a very entertaining structure. Although it takes some time to make, you can use it time after time if you regularly change the flowers, depending on the season.

Strung maize leaves

Fill an elongated zinc container with dry floral foam. Prick pieces of thick wire into the floral foam and stick maize leaves on the wire. Put a floral foam brick on top of the strung structure and fill it with typical autumn materials, e.g. capsules of the yellow flag iris (Iris pseudacorus), Anaphalis, Sedum 'Purple Emperor' and unripe elderberries (Sambucus nigra).

Threaded rhubarb sticks

Thread rhubarb sticks (Rheum rhabar-
barum) with aluminium thread. At the
top, create a Biedermeier arrangement
with roses (Rosa), carnations (Dianthus),
Celosia cristata gr. and beech leaf.

Tip: Use different coloured roses. This will
give the arrangement a much nicer effect.

Playful string draped over dish

Perforate the flat, black, round shells with a sharp object and string the shells on a metal wire. Fill the dish with floral foam and lay the long string on the dish. Secure the string onto the floral foam with long mossing pins. Stick small tubes on top of the dish and between the shells and fill them with Helleborus flowers. Arrange Icelandic moss and pepper balls between the shells to finish.

1 | Bending

Bending is very common in flower arranging, especially in woven and braided structures. It can also be applied without the need to work in two directions. You can bend branches from one side to another, e.g. in floral foam. You can also bend materials by threading them, by wrapping them in metal wire ...

Bent spring

Clasp small glass bottles in the accordion of branches. Bend tulips and birch branches and join them together with floral foam bind wire.

Bent structure

Fill a dish with wet floral foam and cut the foam to the same height of the dish. Bend flexible green Cornus branches from one side to the other. Bend Zantedeschias with different lengths toward each other and arrange the Passiflora vines on top. Cover the bottom of the dish with ball moss and the sides with flat moss.

Tip: You can make the stems flexible by soaking them in water for a few hours.

Bent Allium

Wrap a polystyrene wreath with butterbur (Petasites hybridus) using mossing pins. Place the wreath on top of a water-filled bowl and put the stems of the Allium flowers in the bowl. Bend the stems in a nice shape onto the wreath, starting from the centre. Fix them by pinning the stems.

2 | Hanging

Hanging is a great, alternative technique to decorate high spaces or to make arrangements with beautiful materials that can be hung on a structure. One of the conditions is to use materials that need no water, unless you put them in tubes. You can hang materials by fastening a thread to the petiole, by wrapping and hanging the materials or using hooks which you attach to the materials.

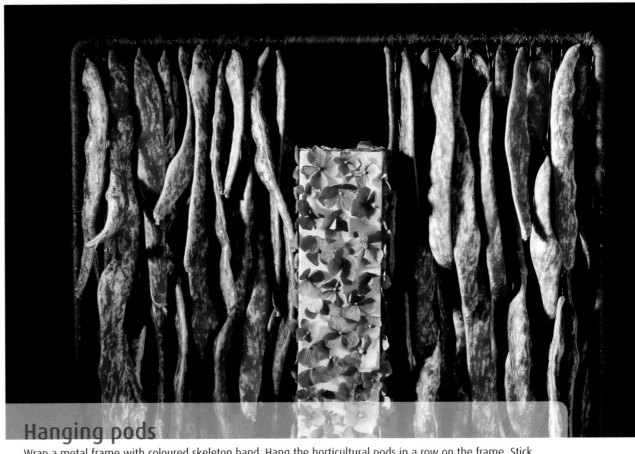

Hanging pods

Wrap a metal frame with coloured skeleton band. Hang the horticultural pods in a row on the frame. Stick individual hydrangea flowers (Hydrangea macrophylla) to a block of colourful floral foam and hang it in the middle of the construction.

3 | Screwing

Screwing is particularly fun when you use branches and dry materials. Dried exotic fruits, stumps and thick branches can be attached to other materials with a screw or several screws. Over the past few years there has been a tendency in floral art to use rough, often exotic materials that are perfect for this technique.

Beech branch on shelf

Screw together a beautiful, big, 'fallen' branch onto a shelf. Wrap Narcissus 'Tête à Tête' and Muscari corms individually in a thin moss layer and clasp them between the branches.

Tip: Ideal arrangement for decorating your garden.

4 | Knotting

Knotting is a technique with not so many uses, but it is nevertheless worth mentioning. You can only use it with flexible greens or other natural materials, such as raffia, sisal, etc. Knots can also be a decorative element in an arrangement or used as a method to clasp flowers between any other knotted materials.

Flower container with knots

Fill a glass dish with grass tree (Xanthorrhoea australis). Make knots with bear grass (Xerophyllum tenax) and clasp them on top of the dish. Arrange small Helleborus branches in between.

5│Piling up

Piling up means that you put materials (generally the same kind) on top of each other, arranging flowers, moss, etc. in between. You obviously have to take into account stability. In terms of materials, this technique can be compared to the stringing technique.

Pile of exotic plants

Cut coloured floral foam with a cake-mould into several slices. Pile up the slices and join them with a long, wooden stick. Prick a long, glass test tube into the top slices. This way the flowers get water. Arrange exotic flowers in the tube, such as Heliconias and Alpinas.

6 | Strewing

The strewing technique means that you throw berries, petals, egg shells, etc. around your arrangement. By strewing extra materials — also the ones used in your composition — around the arrangement, you will give it a special added value. This is only possible with materials that last some time without water!

Tools and materials

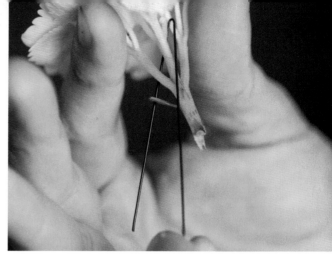

In this chapter we will discuss some useful flower arranging tools and materials. Over the years they have changed quite a lot. One of the most important evolutions has been the invention of floral foam. Originally developed by the firm Smithers-Oasis, this product has brought about a real revolution among florists. Since then the traditional stick bases, including Sphagnum (peat moss), Florapak, clay and flower pricker have almost completely disappeared. Its technical possibilities and ease have made floral foam one of the florist's main materials. As a logical consequence many companies have tried to imitate the original floral foam. However, in this educational context we want to limit ourselves to the OASIS® products because they are guaranteed quality.

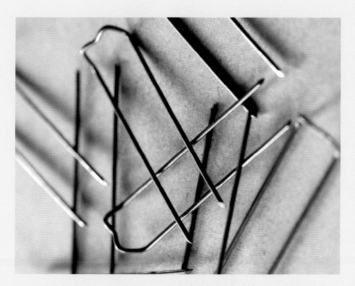

1|Florist scissors, knife, secateur and wire secateur

The florist or potato knife, the florist secateur, the florist scissors and the wire secateur are the florist's basic tools. Flowers stems ought to be cut at an angle with a sharp potato knife. The back of the knife also serves to make perfect, fine hooks in flower thread. Woody plant stems can also be cut at an angle with florist secateur. For the foliage and other green materials, you can use florist scissors. If you need to cut metal thread, you will obviously need the wire secateur.

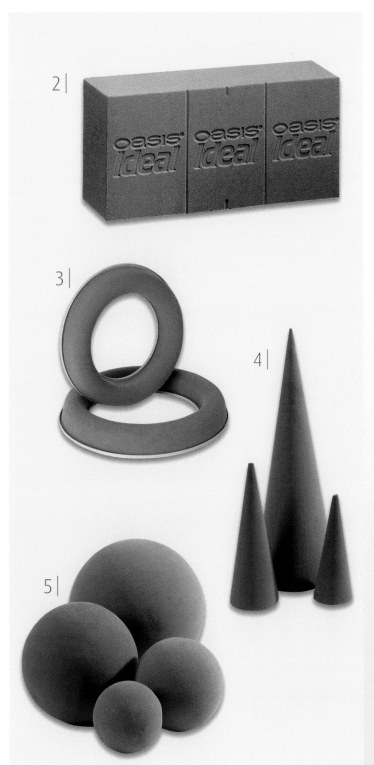

2 | OASIS® bricks

The right way to make floral foam absorb water, is putting it in a washbasin or tub filled with at least 10 cm of water. Just let the block float on the water. After half a minute, it will be totally full of water. Never immerse the block! This causes air bags to form inside the foam structure, which will remain dry, and as a consequence the flowers will not receive any water.

One of the main features of floral foam is that it absorbs water very well, holding it for several days. However, it is still necessary to refill it regularly because the water evaporates off at room temperature. This way, the green material always receives the humidity it needs. Also, it is very easy to stick the stems into the foam and the flowers remain in position.

The bricks are pre-cut into two or three parts. They are easy to cut or model. You can shape the foam perfectly into the desired form by rubbing it with a piece of wet or dry OASIS®.

There are five types of OASIS® floral foam. There is Premium (for delicate arrangements), Ideal (also fit for heavy arrangements) and Economy (the economic version of Ideal). OASIS® Instant and Standard are less known among the general public.

3 | OASIS® rings

OASIS® rings are rings made of floral foam, mounted onto a grey, plastic base. They are the perfect base form for floral wreaths. The rings are available in different sizes (Ø: 15 cm, 20 cm, 25 cm, 30 cm).

4 | OASIS® cones

These cones are also made out of floral foam. They are ideal for higher constructions with a base in which you arrange flowers. Available in different sizes (heights: 24 cm, 32 cm, 40 cm, 50 cm en 60 cm).

5 | OASIS® sphere

Experience shows that it is not always easy to create perfect geometric shapes. Besides the shapes, spheres are another good example. These spheres are made of floral foam. They are available in different sizes (Ø: 9 cm, 12 cm, 16 cm, 20 cm).

1 | Polystyrene cake dummies and spheres

Among the general public polystyrene foam is often called Styropor, after the brand name. It is a synthetic material, originally used as an insulation material in the building industry. It has been used by florists for a long time, but now it is really popular again. Polystyrene is available in different shapes and sizes, which is a good thing because it is difficult to shape unless you have a very sharp knife or a hot-wire cutter. With a hot-wire cutter, you can give the polystyrene the shape you desire. If you use a common knife, you will produce a lot of dust and crumbles, which are difficult to remove.

The cake dummies (Ø: 15 cm, 20 cm, 25 cm, 30 cm; height: 7 cm) and spheres are the most popular shapes. The spheres are available in two versions: either full spheres (Ø: 4-8 cm, 10 cm, 12cm) or hollow half spheres (Ø: 15 cm, 20 cm, 25 cm, 30 cm, 40 cm, 50 cm).

2 | Bridy or bridal bouquet holders

Although many bridal bouquets are still being used in the classical way (using the thread techniques), bouquet holders have become increasingly popular. The reason is pretty obvious: they are very easy to use. They consist of a plastic handle with a removable frame, filled with floral foam. This is especially useful when the floral foam base is broken because the sticking was not done properly and you want to start all over again.

3 | Floral foam pin holders and OASIS® Fix or cling

A wet floral foam brick in an open dish with a smooth surface (e.g. ceramics or glass) tends to slip back and forth. This is obviously something you want to avoid when you create or transport a floral arrangement. To avoid slipping, you can use pin holders and OASIS® Fix. This is an adhesive paste available on one or five meter reels. It is even more adhesive when you warm it up with a flame or by kneading it with your fingers.

What is the right order? After you have warmed up the adhesive or OASIS® Fix, stick it onto the smooth surface. Press the pin holder with the back downwards into the adhesive. Wait a moment and then secure the wet floral foam brick onto the pin holder. OASIS® Fix is also often used to give more stability to candles in taper sticks or candleholders.

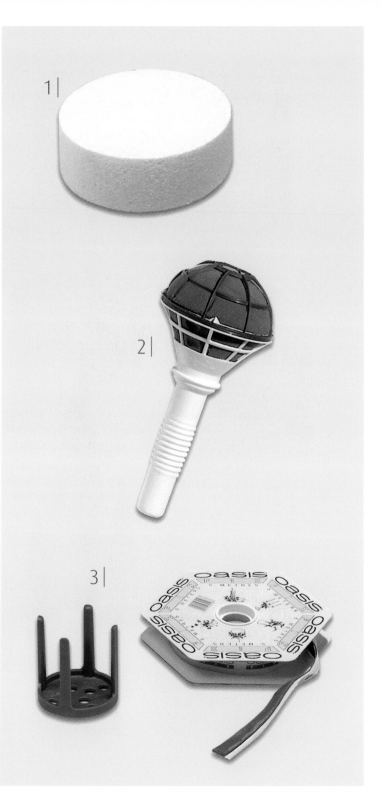

4 | Candleholder

This product is used to easily arrange candles onto a floral foam base. A possible alternative is to use a sharply cut piece of thick floral wire. Warm up the sharp side with a flame and stick it into the bottom of the candle with pliers.

5 | Glue spray

Glue spray is mainly used to secure glitter material or powder snow onto flower arrangements. But you can also use glue spray to give a fixed shape to light materials such as pine needles or light leaves.

6 | Glue gun and glue sticks or silicone cartridges

Glue guns are like soldering bolts in the shape of a gun into which a silicone cartridge is introduced. The point of the silicone is heated and starts melting. You squeeze the melted silicone out of the gun by pulling the trigger. With this hot liquid glue you can attach two or more materials. Once the silicone has cooled down, the materials will remain firmly attached to each other. Use a good glue gun that melts the silicone as quickly as possible. This way, you avoid applying too much pressure on the gun's mechanism. A good glue gun is also designed in such a way, that you won't burn your fingers! Good glue guns are equipped with specially adapted cartridges. Because of the special composition of this silicone, it starts melting at a relatively low temperature and the top of the gun is covered with a special protection lid. Good glue guns are slightly more expensive than common glue guns, but they guarantee good quality.
Glue guns are used in the first place to secure hard materials (nuts, pieces of bark ...) Never use them with soft materials such as foliage or flowers. Other than that, they are not suitable and very hard to use on wet materials.

7 | Cold glue

Although it has been said many times that cold glue will disappear, it always comes back. It is a nearly indispensable product in contemporary floral art. Cold glue is exclusively used to glue soft materials, e.g. leaves, petals, stems ... Cold glue does not contain any aggressive components that may harm the green material and does not scorch the green material, contrary to the glue gun.

1 | Anchor tape or water-resistant tape

Anchor tape is a great kind of adhesive tape. If you want to secure something onto another material and you have good reasons to believe that it will become humid or that humidity will become in between, then you should certainly use anchor tape. This is e.g. the case with funeral wreaths, when you want to place a floral foam brick on top of the wreath to make a nice flower sprig. Attach the brick to the straw wreath by perforating both with two crosswise placed Tonkin sticks. To stabilise and fix the floral foam brick, wrap the anchor tape a few times around the brick and the straw wreath. To avoid the anchor tape cutting too much into the floral foam, place another Tonkin stick on the corresponding edge.

2 | Spool wire

As it name indicates, spool wire is a thin kind of metal wire, wrapped around a plastic spool. It is available in several colours, but the most common colours are still silver and gold. We don't use it that much to bind materials together (unless we use a lot, structured one next to the other) but rather as a decorative element, because of its nice shiny aspect.

3 | Floral ribbon

When you secure flowers or plants with floral wire, e.g. for corsages or bridal arrangements, and you don't want it to be visible, you can wrap the floral wire with ribbon. Start from the crossing point or even a little higher. It is recommended to work by pieces, e.g. using 10 cm of ribbon. Hold the tip against the starting point and tightly wrap the rest of the ribbon around the floral wire, pulling gently.

4 | Pipette tubes and bottles

Sometimes the use of floral foam is not a possible option. Maybe the concept of your arrangement does not allow using floral foam, or maybe there is simply no suitable place to incorporate a wet floral foam base that guarantees a watertight construction. But ... you do want flowers in your arrangement, and flowers need water. How can you do this? The solution is the use of pipette tubes (sometimes called test tubes, according to their original function). These are tubes in transparent synthetic material or glass, sometimes equipped with a rubber cap with a small hole to introduce a stem. For aesthetic reasons it is a good idea to wrap these convenient, synthetic tubes in green material (e.g. leaves or moss). Attach the tube to your arrangement with winding wire, raffia or coloured metal wire.

Filling the tubes is very easy if you use a pipette bottle. A pipette bottle is a little synthetic bottle with a sturdy, bent plastic straw. This way you can easily reach the tube to fill it with water, even when the flower and the tube have already been inserted into the arrangement.

Care of flowers and arrangements

Real flowers are vital for everyone who loves floral arrangements. What is it that makes flowers so beautiful? Why do we love them so much?
Maybe the fact that they are perishable makes them especially attractive. As soon as a flower is harvested, the ageing process starts.
It is a shame, but at the same time it makes real flowers so different from artificial flowers, that always look the same.
Of course you want to enjoy your bouquet as long as possible. After all, you have invested a lot of time and energy in your arrangement.

Some tips to keep your flowers for longer:

· AT THE FLOWER SHOP

It all starts at the flower shop. Does the flower look fresh? Is it solid? How many days has it been blooming? What do the stems look like? What do the leaves look like? And the thorns? What does the water look like where the flowers are?
Never buy unripe flowers. In technical terms we say they were cut early. These flowers will never fully open and wither fast. For the consumer it is not always easy to recognise these flowers.
Buy your flowers from a reputable, professional florist. Besides, shops that buy and sell a lot are in a better position to guarantee the products' freshness.

· TRANSPORT AND PACKING

When you transport flowers, take care of extreme temperatures, never too high or too low.
Take the flowers out of the packing as soon as possible. Flowers that are packed too tightly have a higher risk of fungus infections.

· THE MATERIAL

If you use flowers from your own garden, you can be totally certain that they are fresh. Make sure they are sufficiently ripe when you cut them. The best moment for harvesting is early in the morning. During the night flowers absorb a lot of water. If you buy flowers, leave them in water for a few hours, especially if you are going to arrange them in floral foam. Once the arrangement is ready, it is important to regularly add some water to the floral foam.
Make a slanted cut at a 45° angle. Always remove excessive or damaged leaves. In the case of flowers like gladiolus or freesia it is important to remove the smallest buds. They usually don't open and

consume much of the plant's energy, to the expense of the other buds. Immediately remove faded flowers from their bouquet or other arrangements.

Some flowers loose sap (e.g. Euphorbia, Papaver). It may sound contradictory but we recommend searing up the stems immediately after cutting in order to stimulate the water absorption and to avoid the stem from bleeding to death. There are two methods to do this: submerge the stem for a few seconds in hot water (minimum 60 °C/ 140 °F) or keep it under a burning candle.

Always use clean buckets and vases. Calcium stains on glass can easily be removed with vinegar. Don't put them in too much or too little water. About 4-5 inches is perfect.

Add cut flower food to the vase water and to the water you use to wet the floral foam. Flowers start ageing from the moment they are cut. Cut flower food slows down this process (feeding, protection against bacteria ...). The grower, wholesaler and retailer all use these products. It is important that you, as a consumer, continue this process. This way you will keep your flowers nicer for longer. There are many kinds of cut flower food. Some are for general use, others are very specific. Choose the right cut flower food (e.g. Chrysal) for the different kinds of flowers you use. Respect the quantities indicated on the packing.

· THE ENVIRONMENT

Create the ideal environment for your flowers. Smoke, draughts and too much direct sunlight will damage your flowers. If the air is too humid, this will boost the development of fungus infections. Do not place your flowers near ripe fruit, because they do not like the ethylene, released by the ripening fruit. Place them at a cool spot in the evening. This will increase their lifetime considerably.

And above all: CHERISH YOUR FLOWERS!

About colours and their use

Colours and colour combinations play an essential role in flower arranging. Many people think choosing a colour or colour combination is a difficult task. You need to feel the colour and develop the ability to combine them. Depending on the colour combinations you choose, your arrangement will radiate harmony ... or disharmony.

On the next pages you will find a few practical principles of chromatics, but as people always say ... there is no accounting for tastes — or colours!

The colour circles:

We all know Newton's, Oswald's and Itten's colour circles from our art classes at school. They give a good view of the different kinds of colours and can help you when choosing colours or making a combination.

Complementary colours:
Colours that are each other's opposites. They are across each other in the colour circle. The result is fairly harsh.

Harmonising colours:
Colours that look nice when they are combined.

Tone-on-tone or co-ordinated colours:
The same colours are used, but with a slightly different shade.

Pastel shades:
Colours that contain a lot of white (soft shades).

Disharmonising colours:
Colours that don't match each other. They are on both sides of the colours blue and red, e.g. cornflower blue versus lilac blue. Other combinations that usually don't look good are primary colours with a pastel shade of a different primary colour.

Warm colours:
Or active colours, e.g. red, orange, yellow. These colours come to the foreground in an arrangement.

Cold colours:
Or passive colours, e.g. blue, purple. They are not very eye-catching and tend to keep in the background. They create a sensation of rest, although they feel rather cool.

Neutral colours:
Colours like pure green, white and black. Really black flowers do not exist. Although we speak of e.g. black tulips, the truth is they are dark brown or dark purple.

Colour contrast:
The biggest colour contrast is reached by combining colours that are straight across from each other in the colour circle. This combination is only for people who like to take risks!

Tips:
It is important that you feel comfortable with your colour choice. The colour choice must harmonise with the environment where you will place or hang the arrangement.

Colours are often related to a certain style. With pastel shades you make romantic arrangements. Bright red and white are suitable for a beautiful, tight, contemporary floral creation.

The time of the year will influence the colour choice and the offer. In summer and autumn you can find the greatest variety of colours. I like to create autumn combinations with salmon pink, yellow and burgundy. In spring, I feel like using totally different colours. You can obtain surprising effects by lighting the arrangement. The kind of lighting is crucial to show the colours in all their splendour.

Obviously trends are very important and often go hand in hand with fashion. Some years everybody goes exuberant, in other periods simple and sober colours are the rule.

Remember you will never get it wrong with a white and green combination. It fits into any home and everybody likes it.

For religious arrangements you should take into account the corresponding colours: white for birth and baptism, red for confirmation, etc. For a wedding the typical colour is white, although recently people have also started to use other colours. The colours depend on the bridal gown and the bridesmaids' dresses. They are usually also determined by the bride's favourite flowers.

Flower arranging styles

From the many possibilities in flower arranging a wide range of styles have been developed, going from classical to modern. All flower creations are variations on a certain style, using one or several techniques.

Whereas in the past style was the main aspect of the arrangement, the past few years technique has gained more importance at the moment of watching and assessing a flower creation.

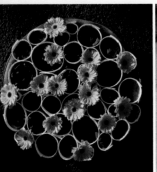   

Western flower arranging

We can distinguish between western and eastern styles.
In western arranging there are three kinds of styles:

· The triangle arrangement, the half-round symmetrical arrangement (e.g. Biedermeier), the fan-shape, the S-line ... are examples of the classical style. Many of these arrangements are still being used, but the materials and material combinations have changed.

· Modern arrangements became very popular from the second half of the 20th century onwards. All contemporary arrangements with plant materials, in all kinds of varieties, belong to this category: the decorative, parallel and linear arrangement, woven structures, bound structures ...

· The experimental work is something new. Often these arrangements are not new from the formal point of view, but for their use of secondary materials, originating from other sectors, such as extra fast plaster (building sector) or nori, the seaweed sheets used in the preparation of sushi (culinary sector).

Ikebana or the Japanese art of flower arranging

Ikebana is steeped in eastern culture. For centuries the custom of offering flowers during religious ceremonies developed a whole range of different styles that cannot be found in any other culture. Initially subject to strict rules, today ikebana is a living art that evolves with modern time and lifestyle.

In Japan there are many different schools with branches all over the world. The most important schools are *Ikenobo, Ohara, Sogetsu, Ichyo* and *Saga*. Every school has its own stylistic features.

Eastern and western schools have influenced each other for many decades.

Technique:

For vase arrangements all schools use supporting sticks that secure the branches and flowers in the vase in an invisible way and help to give them the right direction.

In flat dishes the elements are pricked onto a *kenzan*. A *kenzan* (pin holder) is a leaden plate or block with sharp needle-like copper nails. In unusual containers or dishes with an inwards folded edge, clasping techniques are used.

Characteristics:

In traditional styles the asymmetric triangle is very common and open spaces are very important.

In contemporary arrangements the triangles have disappeared, but asymmetry, open spaces, rhythm and the limited variety of materials are maintained.

In experimental arrangements the artist is given complete freedom.

Some history

Man started using plants, and particularly herbs and flowers, in the first place in ritual acts. Traces of this use can be found in diverse religions, among other reasons because religion and healing used to be closely connected. This was already the case in the first civilisations, in the Middle East and Egypt. Flowers and herbs were especially used in bouquets and monumental masonry. At the Olympic Games in Ancient Greece, olive wreaths and flower garlands played an important role.

In the Middle Ages flowers became increasingly popular in secular circles, especially among sovereigns, nobles and merchants. Flowers and fruit were often used to decorate tables. The supply and the interest in plants and flowers grew constantly. The rise of international seagoing made them a genuine trade product. A good example are the bulbs that were brought to Europe by the Venetian merchants in the 16th century and later on via the United Dutch East-Indian Company. This also explains the importance of the Dutch ornamental plant cultivation.

In the late Baroque, from 1700 onwards, many decorative artists exuberantly used the flowers that had found their way to Europe and that were now also cultivated here: Delphinums, peonies, tulips, dahlias, roses ... were richly exhibited and represented. Later, by the influence of rich plant collectors and plant hunters, more and more tropical and subtropical plants and flowers could be found in the West-European orangeries of the rich bourgeoisie and landed nobility. Very often the chatelains' gardeners not only dedicated themselves to the maintenance of the greenery and the plant gardens, but also composed exuberant flower arrangements. A nice example of the growing interaction between the local chatelains and their gardeners is the creation of the *Gentse Floraliën*, the flower show in the Belgian city of Ghent. It still plays an important role in the promotion of the internationally renowned Belgian ornamental plant cultivation. Some styles from that period have wonderfully survived the passing of time. The Biedermeier style, for example, that dates from 1820–1850, is still very important and alive today. One of its characteristics, the typical, compact, decorative arrangement, has influenced the work of many florists, even today.

In the Victorian period (± 1850–1900) ladies started to use more and more floral wreaths, corsages, dresses with garlands, bouquets in their hands, etc. Parties became flower parties. In the 19th century bridal bouquets and accessories became increasingly important. The florist's activity became a real profession and the first flower shops as we know them today, were opened.

The history of flower arranging is different for each and every country. Today there are still countries where it is not very developed. Japan, the Netherlands and Germany have played a pioneers' role for many years. France and the Scandinavian countries are currently experiencing a revival. But the real trendsetter of the past few years is Belgium — and particularly Flanders. The Belgian style and combinations are highly appreciated all over the world. The fact that Belgian and Dutch flower magazines and books are translated into all the languages of the world, are a clear evidence of this phenomenon.

Thank you

Together with my husband Nico Bostoen, I run the school 'De Groene Verbeelding'. He has always encouraged me to take new initiatives. Without him I would have never started this school and I wouldn't have had that many opportunities to work on this dream. He's also my critic par excellence. It's a unique situation when you're able to discuss both the contents and the shape of your work with your partner. This book is yet another project we worked on together. A project which we can proudly call our work, a reflection of what we stand for.

Nico, many, many thanks. I realise that in the future — because of your own professional interests — you won't be as available for our business as you have been in the past. However, I know for sure that you will always be there to support me in my passion.

Spread over 14 months we have worked together with Isabelle Persyn, who has become our good friend-photographer. Time and again she manages to exactly capture the image I had in my head. A very big thank you for your incredible patience, professionalism and friendship.

We'd also like to thank our publishing house Stichting Kunstboek for the opportunity they've given us. By being able to make this book I have certainly grown, which also benefits our school. Many thanks to An Theunynck for her good advise, her help in finding the interesting topics and for rereading our texts. As before, it has been a great cooperation.

Furthermore we would like to thank the board and staff members of Smithers-Oasis for supplying technical information and didactic material (www.smithersoasis.com).

And last, but certainly not least, I would also like to thank all our students for their years of support, for believing in us, for attending our classes and also for being an inspiration.

For this book, we would like to especially thank Agnes Agnessi, Marie-Louise Bollaert, Liliane Droesbeke, Els Struyven, Véronique Peen of Découverte, Lieve Dubois, Lucie Delmeiren, Jeanine Moerman Godelieve Vandenheuvel, Frieda Fierens, Chris Blaze, Lena Verhenne and Monique Roegiers.

Authors:
Gudrun Cottenier and Nico Bostoen
Flower arranging school 'De Groene Verbeelding'
Keirestraat 24
B-9700 Mater (Oudenaarde)
Tel. & Fax +32 55 45 55 25
www.degroeneverbeelding.com (for information and course programms)
info@degroeneverbeelding.com

Creations:
Gudrun Cottenier

Photography:
Isabelle Persyn

Translation:
Taal-Ad-Visië, Brugge (B)

Final editing:
An Theunynck, Femke De Lameillieure

Layout, colour separation and print:
Graphic Group Van Damme bvba, Oostkamp (B)

Published by:
Stichting Kunstboek bvba
Legeweg 165
B-8020 Oostkamp
Tel. +32 50 46 19 10
Fax +32 50 46 19 18
www.stichtingkunstboek.com
info@stichtingkunstboek.com

ISBN: 978-90-5856-221-0
D/6407/2007/10
NUR: 421

Imprint